A Note to Parents and Teachers

Dorling Kindersley Readers is a compelling new reading programme for children, designed in conjunction with leading literacy experts, including Cliff Moon M.Ed., Honorary Fellow of the University of Reading. Cliff Moon has spent many years as a teacher and teacher educator specializing in reading and has written more than 140 books for children and teachers. He reviews regularly for teachers' journals.

Beautiful illustrations and superb full-colour photographs combine with engaging, easy-to-read stories to offer a fresh approach to each subject in the series. Each *Dorling Kindersley Reader* is guaranteed to capture a child's interest while developing his or her reading skills, general knowledge, and love of reading.

The four levels of *Dorling Kindersley Readers* are aimed at different reading abilities, enabling you to choose the books that are exactly right for each child:

Level 1 – Beginning to read
Level 2 – Beginning to read alone
Level 3 – Reading alone
Level 4 – Proficient readers

The "normal" age at which a child begins to read can be anywhere from three to eight years old, so these levels are intended only as a general guideline.

No matter which level you select, you can be sure that you are helping children learn to read, then read to learn!

LONDON, NEW YORK, MUNICH, PARIS,
MELBOURNE, DELHI

Editors Jennifer Siklós and Caroline Bingham
Designer Michelle Baxter
Senior Editor Linda Esposito
Deputy Managing Art Editor Jane Horne
Production Kate Oliver
Photography Richard Leeney
Reading Consultant
Cliff Moon M.Ed.

Published in Great Britain by
Dorling Kindersley Limited
80 The Strand, London WC2R 0RL
A Penguin Company

4 6 8 10 9 7 5

Copyright © 1998 Dorling Kindersley Limited, London

A CIP catalogue record for this book is
available from the British Library.

ISBN 0-7513-5739-1

Colour reproduction by Colourscan, Singapore
Printed and bound in China by L Rex

The publisher would like to thank the following for their kind permission
to reproduce their photographs: Key: t=top, b=below, l=left, r=right, c=centre
Pictor International: (14-15) Jacket: **Pictor International:** front (background)
Additional photography by Andy Crawford (26bl & 32 bolt), Ray Moller (30-31) and Alex Wilson (13t).

All other images © Dorling Kindersley.
For further information see: www.dkimages.com

The publisher would also like to thank Rick Roberton at Western Truck Limited.
Special thanks to John Scholey at W Scholey & Son for the use of his truck, time and premises.

see our catalogue at
www.dk.com

DORLING KINDERSLEY *READERS*

BEGINNING TO READ
1

Truck Trouble

BE-16-88

Written by Angela Royston

John got up very early
to make a special delivery.
He climbed up two steps
into his big blue truck.

John looked at the map.
He had no time to get lost!
Then he started the truck,
checked the mirrors and set off.

mirror

At the service station,
John checked the engine.
It needed some oil.
Then he filled up the fuel tank.

fuel tank

He looked at
the shiny engine.
"Don't let me down!"
he said.
"I can't be late!"

Next he had to pick up his load.
A fork-lift truck lifted big boxes
into the back of John's truck.

There were also some small boxes
marked "Special Delivery".
John put these in the truck too.

John was in a hurry
but he was also
very hungry.

He pulled into a rest area
for breakfast.

John's friend Paul arrived
in his milk tanker.
He joined John for breakfast.

John couldn't stop for long.
He had two deliveries to make.

John drove onto the motorway.
It was jammed with traffic.
Cars and trucks beeped their horns.

John had to deliver the big boxes
to a nearby factory.
He left the motorway
at the next exit.

John waved to the workers as he drove into the factory.

The workers helped him
to unload the big boxes.

"I'm in a hurry,"
John told them.
"I've got another delivery
to make."
He was soon on his way.
But there was trouble ahead!

A van had broken down!
John slammed on the brakes and
his truck screeched to a halt.

The road was very narrow.
John's truck was too wide
to get past the van.

John used his radio to call for help.
He also warned other drivers
to stay away from that road.

Soon John saw flashing lights.
It was a tow truck!
The tow truck
towed the van
to a garage.

flashing
lights

When the road was clear
John hurried on his way.
But there was more trouble ahead!

Boom! Boom!

John drove into a thunderstorm.

Rain began to pour down.

John turned on
the windscreen wipers.

wiper

He drove very slowly.

"This isn't my day!"

he groaned.

John drove on and on.
At last the rain stopped and
he pulled over to eat his lunch.

Then he rested
on a bunk
in the back of the cab.
He fell fast asleep!

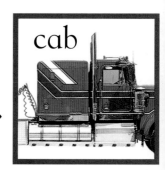

cab

When he woke up, John thought,
"Now I'm in trouble!"

John drove off. BANG!
"Oh no! A flat tyre!"
He grabbed
his tools and
the spare wheel.

wheel

John unscrewed
the bolts and
took off the wheel.

bolt

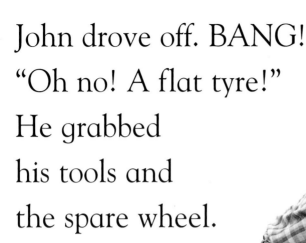

Then he put on the spare wheel.
It was very hard work!

John drove into town.
He had to wait for
a set of traffic lights
to turn green.

traffic
lights

BE-16-88

"Hurry up!" thought John.
It was time to make
his special delivery.

John arrived at last.
There was no time to spare!
He unloaded the boxes marked
"Special Delivery".

John was just in time for the party at the new children's hospital.

Inside the special boxes
were piles of toys.
"Thank you!" shouted the children.
"It was no trouble!" said John.

Picture Word List

mirror
page 7

cab
page 24

fuel tank
page 9

wheel
page 26

flashing
lights
page 21

bolt
page 26

wiper
page 23

traffic
lights
page 28